THE PIKE COUNTY BALLADS

The Pike County Ballads

Illustrated by

N. C. WYETH

Reprinted by
James Stevenson Publisher
Fairfield, California
www.jspub.com

James Stevenson Publisher, holder of copyright © 2004, of introductions by Wayne Temple, Paul Findley, and Warren Winston to Pike County Ballads.

ISBN 1-885852-25-8

Library of Congress Control Number: 2002102907

Historical copyright record:
1871 and 1890 by John Hay

1912 edition illustrated by N.C. Wyeth
by Houghton Mifflin Company

Contents and Illustrations

Introductory Perspectives

John Hay, Author and Statesman 9
    by Wayne Temple
A Curious Twist of History 21
    by Paul Findley
Pike County Folks in John Hay's Dialect Poems. 27
    by Warren Winston
Publisher's Message 33
    by James Stevenson

Pike County Ballads

Illustrator's Preface 43
    by N. C. Wyeth
Jim Bludso 45
He were n't no saint, — them engineers
  Is all pretty much alike
Little Breeches 51
No four-year-old in the county
  Could beat him for pretty and strong
Banty Tim 57
But he staggered up, and packed me off,
  With a dozen stumbles and falls
The Mystery of Gilgal 63
I ax yer parding, Mister Phinn —
  Jest drap that whisky-skin
Golyer 71
Over hill and holler and ford and creek
  Jest like the hosses had wings, we tore
The Pledge at Spunky Point 77
The Deacon and Parson Skeeters
  In the tail of a game of Draw

THE PIKE COUNTY BALLADS

John Hay: Author and Statesman

JOHN Milton Hay was born on October 12, 1838, in Salem, Washington County, Indiana, a very small town in the southern part of the state. His parents were Dr. Charles and Helen (Leonard) Hay. Dr. Hay, a physician and a Freemason, moved his little family to Warsaw, Hancock County, Illinois, in 1841. For much better schooling, Dr. Hay sent John southeast to a private academy in Pittsfield, Pike County, Illinois, where he lived with Attorney Milton Hay, his uncle. While in Pittsfield, he made the acquaintance of John George Nicolay (1832-1901), a newspaper editor, and also observed other interesting residents of that county-seat town. Some of them most certainly became the prototypes for the characters mentioned by Hay in his later writings, including *The Pike County Ballads and Other Pieces*.

To continue his formal education beyond the

academy, John M. Hay, who stemmed from a family of means, migrated eastward to Springfield, Illinois, where he received board and room in the home of his grandfather, John Hay (1775-1865), the brick maker and business man. Young John had taken up residence in the Capital city to attend the new Illinois State University which had just opened that April of 1852. Classes first met in the old First Presbyterian Church building at Third and Washington streets. But alas, it was not a large "state" institution, and it certainly was not a "university." Actually, it was a small private college where Hay became friends with little Robert Todd Lincoln (1843-1926), then just eleven years of age and enrolled in the Preparatory Department.

Hay, a voracious reader on his own, also studied the classics, learned foreign languages and received a sufficiently advanced education so as to graduate in 1855. He proceeded as a sophomore to

JOHN HAY: AUTHOR AND STATEMAN

Brown University, a Baptist institution at Providence, Rhode Island. A brilliant student and the Class Poet, he graduated in 1858 with distinction and a gold Phi Beta Kappa key.

After a long rest at the home of his parents, Hay returned to Springfield in the spring of 1859 to study law with Milton Hay (1817-1893) in the firm of Hay, Campbell & Cullom on the East side of the Public Square. Milton Hay had obtained his law license on June 24, 1840, and had come back to Springfield from Pittsfield shortly before his nephew's arrival. Young John took up residence with grandfather John and with Milton Hay at the home they shared on the Southeast corner of Second and Jefferson streets. Milton Hay was trained in law by the preceptor method in the noted firm of Stuart & Lincoln. Milton had set up a cot in the law office (ca. 1839) while the senior partner John Todd Stuart, was away in Congress and often invited Lincoln out to the brick kilns of the senior John Hay where they roasted potatoes and chickens in the torrid heat of the furnaces. These kilns had produced all the bricks laid into the interior walls, etc, of the Capitol Building on the Square. Through the two older Hays, young John renewed his contact with Abraham Lincoln and also renewed his friendship with John G. Nicolay who at that time was the Chief Clerk to Ozias Mather Hatch, the Illinois Secretary of State, also from Griggsville, Pike County.

When Abraham Lincoln was nominated by the Republicans for President on May 18, 1860, in Chicago, he needed a suitable office in Springfield to conduct the affairs of his new station in life. Governor John Wood offered him the use of his office and reception room on the second floor in the State House. To secure a secretary, Lincoln simply walked down to the northwest corner of the first floor in the Capitol and asked J.G. Nicolay to fill that position. Nicolay quickly agreed but soon discovered that the labors were overwhelming him. So, he begged his friend, John Hay, to leave his law books and assist him.

Almost immediately after Lincoln was nominated, John Hay began to pen news articles, mostly for out-of-town newspapers. His first known article was written on May 21, 1860. He was a brilliant author and could give Lincoln's opinions and thoughts without the candidate having to put his own name to them. In fact, Hay also wrote under an assumed name. However, his flowery prose contained foreign words and phrases and mentioned figures in mythology and history that the less-educated, general-reading public perhaps could not appreciate or even understand.

After Lincoln won the election, he implored Nicolay to accompany him to Washington as his private secretary, whereupon Nicolay told him that Hay should go, also, although there was no salary provided by law for an assistant secretary. At first Lincoln quipped that he could not take all of Springfield along with him. Yet he finally relented and offered Hay a secretarial job which Hay quickly accepted, much to the disappointment and worry of his father, Charles, who must have envisioned a more steady and professional occupation in the law for his talented son. What would John do without a law license after his political work ended?

To insure that John Hay would have a legal practice to fall back upon after his prestigious stint at the White House, powerful Springfieldians—most certainly including President-elect Lincoln—saw to it that John passed the "examination" and was admitted to the Illinois Bar on February 4, 1861, just one week before the Presidential Special pulled out of Springfield with Nicolay and Hay aboard. All along the route to Washington, John Hay indited colorful and insightful dispatches for the press. He spent hours at this task which kept the public well informed of the progress of the train. These articles proved to be most valuable for later researchers and historians, and Hay's purple prose grew less obnoxious and pedantic. He was learning very slowly.

Once in the White House, President Lincoln secured a salary for Hay in another department which then assigned him to the Executive Mansion. With Robert away at Harvard, President Lincoln grew quite fond of Hay and seems to have treated him like his own son. But Hay put on airs which irritated some folks. On one occasion, Hay boasted, "Yes, I'm Keeper of the President's Conscience." One thing he did keep was his informative diary and his continuing personal letters and public dispatches for the press, unsigned, of course as to the latter.

Perhaps to avoid the charge of a "ghost payroller" in one of his departments, Lincoln had John Hay commissioned a Major as an Assistant Adjutant General on January 12, 1864. From then on he drew Army pay until he mustered out on April 8, 1867 as a Colonel. On one of his trips back to Springfield, Miss Anna Ridgley noted in her diary on June 21, 1864, that Major Hay had appeared on the streets in his field-grade uniform. He strutted around town and talked in the most affected manner possible. Yes, nobody ever accused the callow young Mr. Hay as being overly modest. He tended to be quite dapper, priggish, given to snide remarks and stilted prose. Mrs. Lincoln grew to detest him thoroughly when he would not go along with her little schemes to acquire money in an illegal manner. Honesty was one of Hay's virtues along with his literary skills, and it certainly cost him his White House position.

Hay was a gay blade in Washington society, and he continued to write voluminously. Charles Henry Philbrick (1837-1885), an honor graduate of Illinois college in Jacksonville and a resident of Griggsville, labored as an assistant secretary to Lin-

JOHN HAY: AUTHOR AND STATEMAN

coln from September 14, 1864, until the President's death. He left some personal observations of Major Hay and Mr. Nicolay. Often Hay remained closeted in "his private room" while the staff worked away on the mountain of paperwork. "Nicolay," disclosed Philbrick, "is gloomy on account of physical and mental trouble. I think if he and I could make an 'even divide,' he taking a part of my 163 lbs. weight, and giving me some of his indifference and industry, that we should each be the better for the bargain. Hay does the *ornamental*...and the main labor is divided between three others of us who manage to get along tolerably well with it."

Nevertheless, John Hay did "ornamentally" compose one of the greatest letters to bear President Lincoln's signature. That was the note of condolence to Lydia Bixby, November 21, 1864. Dr. Michael Burlingame has proved beyond doubt that Hay's fluid pen set it down on paper. A computer check has confirmed that the words and style are Hay's, not Lincoln's. Here is the long closing sentence. "I pray that our Heavenly Father may assuage the anguish of your bereavement, and leave you only the cherished memory of the loved and lost, and the solemn pride that must be yours, to have laid so costly a sacrifice upon the altar of Freedom." That is a masterpiece resulting from a classical education at Brown.

At the beginning of Lincoln's second term of office, he decided to send Nicolay to Paris to head the U.S. Legation there, and Hay went as Secretary to the Legation. Hay remained in Europe, serving not only in Paris but also Madrid and Vienna. Upon returning to the United States, he obtained an editorship on the staff of the New York Tribune, writing numerous stories and books, including *The Pike County Ballads* and *Castillian Days*, both in 1871. His many journal articles and magazine tales also won wide approval, and he settled down into a reserved, polished gentleman who often regretted his flamboyant airs and cutting remarks of the past.

JOHN HAY: AUTHOR AND STATEMAN

Hay resigned from the Tribune, and on February 4, 1874, married Miss Clara Louise Stone, daughter of the wealthy Amasa Stone of Cleveland, Ohio. For a number of years he became part of Stone's financial empire, but with a very wealthy wife decided to return to politics and writing. He went to Washington, D.C., where he became the Assistant Secretary of State on November 1, 1879. During these years, he started to write a ten volume life of Lincoln; Nicolay was the coauthor of the very popular *Abraham Lincoln: A History*, published in 1890. Robert T. Lincoln allowed them access to all of President Lincoln's papers and looked over their shoulders while they were composing it. It might be termed "an authorized biography."

Hay's political star then rose rapidly. From 1897 to 1898 he was Ambassador to England, then from 1898 to 1901 he was chosen Secretary of State under President William McKinley. He continued in that post under President Theodore Roosevelt, from

THE PIKE COUNTY BALLADS

1901 to 1905. Never of a strong physical makeup, Hay died in office on July 1, 1905. He is buried in Lake View Cemetery at Cleveland, Ohio.

      Wayne C. Temple

      Springfield, Illinois

      December, 2004

A Curious Twist of History

JOHN Hay's service as Secretary of State in the administration of President Theodore Roosevelt, caused him to act as primary negotiator of the treaty that established U.S. control of the Panama Canal Zone. Earlier he had served as ambassador to Great Britain. He had served with distinction, however, late in his career he was embarrassed to be known as the author of the *The Pike County Ballads*. He wanted them forgotten.

In a curious twist of history, Hay may be better known today for the ballads than for his remarkable diplomatic achievements. They provide a unique, intimate glimpse of the life, language and spirit of mid-America during the Civil War period. In the preface, illustrator N. C. Wyeth paints a word sketch of the ballads that is just as robust and beautiful as his paint-

THE PIKE COUNTY BALLADS

ings that bring vividly to life the ballad characters and their surroundings.

This book presents life along the Mississippi River in powerful, concise imagery that, to my knowledge, is unmatched in any other literature. The language is as unkempt and, at times, as raw as river life must have been.

The words are preserved in this special edition without alteration. Nigger—a word that I detest—appears, but it must be read in the context of American society of the times, and especially in the atmosphere created by the ballads themselves. Today, the "n" word is almost always used as a demeaning insult, epithet or taunt, but when the ballads were written, it was used as a slang version of the word Negro.

Can anyone read "Banty Tim," the "n" word notwithstanding, without deep rejoicing in Sergeant Tilmon Joy's powerful stand against those who would

A CURIOUS TWIST OF HISTORY

run African-American Tim out of "white man's country?"

When the ballads were written, the ink on the Emancipation Proclamation was scarcely dry, and most white people, sadly, accepted the false notion that black people are inherently inferior intellectually. Two generations later, for example, this calumny was accepted as truthful by people as scholarly as Woodrow Wilson.

During my twenty-two years as a Member of Congress, I encountered bigotry aplenty on Capitol Hill. I proudly supported all civil rights bills that came before Congress, but I knew that racism cannot be legislated out of existence. Sadly, it still exists. Our nation has come a long way, but racial discrimination still stains the American dream.

The Pike County Ballads chronicle a period of some advance in race relations, but they tell *much* more. They portray life on river banks in early Amer-

THE PIKE COUNTY BALLADS

ica. I have special affection for Hay's poems, because our family had the joy of living for fourteen wonderful years in Pike County, the site of the ballads, where rivers are still a vital part of everyday living. We gloried in the knowledge that Hay spent more than a year in Pike County where he first heard tales that inspired his poetry. And it was in Pike County that he made the acquaintance of a local weekly newspaper editor, John G. Nicolay, an immigrant from Bavaria.

The ballads first came to my attention in 1948. As the newly hired manager of the weekly *Pike County Republican,* I took notes as Democrat Paul H. Douglas, soon to be elected to the U.S. Senate, spoke from the steps of the courthouse in Pittsfield, the seat of Pike County government. During his talk, to my surprise, Douglas recited "Banty Tim" from memory. From that day forward, although a Republican, I was

A CURIOUS TWIST OF HISTORY

a Douglas fan—and a Hay fan too. When you read the ballad, you too may commit it to memory.

        Paul Findley

        Jacksonville, Illinois

        December 2004

THE PIKE COUNTY BALLADS

Pike County Folks in John Hay's Dialect Poems

AT the request of James Stevenson Publisher, I have assembled bits and pieces of information from various sources to provide background information about the characters found in *The Pike County Ballads* – which Hay called "dialect poems."

John Hay was about three years of age when his parents moved from Indiana to Warsaw, Illinois, a short distance north of Pike County. When he was old enough, young John went to live with his uncle, Attorney Milton Hay, where he entered Thomson Academy in Pittsfield, Illinois to continue his education. Pittsfield, where Lincoln practiced law, was the seat of Pike County government.

In these formative years young John observed the "rugged frontier types depicted in Pike County Ballads." A.S. Chapman's article, "The Boyhood of John Hay" found in an old issue of "The Century

THE PIKE COUNTY BALLADS

Magazine" reports that much of the population of Pike County came from Virginia, Kentucky and Tennessee and therefore had Southern sympathies, hence the conflict between Tilmon Joy and the White Man's Committee found in Banty Tim was representative of the divisions in Pike County in the years following the Civil War.

There is no mystery about the Tilmon Joy character in "Banty Tim." My fellow Lincoln historian and friend, Michael Burlingame, wrote in a footnote in his *With Lincoln in the White House, Letters, Memoranda, and Other Writings of John G. Nicolay, 1860-1865*, "Therena Bates of Pittsfield, Illinois...wed Nicolay.... Her brother, Dorus E. Bates, was a blacksmith who served as a captain in the Union Army, lost an arm at Vicksburg, and became the model for Tilmon Joy in John Hay's poem, 'Banty Tim.'" Bates' heroism in the battle of Vicksburg was well known during the Civil War era in Pike County,

Illinois. He was a hero whose story would certainly have been known to Nicolay and his young friend and colleague John Hay. As for "Spunky Point," Warsaw, in which Hay had lived as a young boy, was known as Spunky Point by early residents.

In "The Pledge at Spunky Point," there appears to be a composite of several characters. The name "Fry" is found in the area – a Frye family ran a mill at Big Blue Creek. Esteemed Carthage attorney Franklin Hartzell recalls the late Leon Lamet, a Warsaw attorney, saying, "In the Warsaw area there was a family named Golliher." There was also a James Gallaher who could have been John Hay's Golyer, and, of course, there was Dorus Bates' "Tilmon Joy." These men and others "signed the pledge for to drink no more that year."

For the character Jim Bludso, of the Prairie Belle, Mr. Hartzell states that in the 1859 Plat Book, the Bledsoes' owned a farm in Wilcox Township, south of Warsaw. Near the farm is a river crossing and a navigation light known as the Bledsoe crossing light. According to Lamet, Hay would have been acquainted with the Bledsoe family of Hancock County, and that is where he got "Jim Bludso".

"Little Breeches," according to Chapman in his "Century Magazine" article, "was a story related as fact by a Baptist minister in a sermon "Special Providence" preached at Warsaw when John Hay was a boy, and the story stayed in his mind 'til his fancy worked it into rhyme.

"Gilgal," Chapman tells us, "was an actual settlement on the Mississippi River, the shipping-point for Rockport, where there was a large mill, and for Atlas and other inland towns. The combination of grocery and groggery was not unusual in river towns, and was the natural meeting-place for fire-eaters like Judge Phinn and Colonel Blood." In the ballad, "The Mystery of Gilgal," Judge Phinn might have been a Griggsville resident, by the name of Shinn. Colonel

PIKE COUNTY FOLKS

Blood was perhaps the Captain Blood, also of Griggsville. In ante bellum Griggsville feelings ran high between abolitionists and pro-slavery advocates. With townsfolk meeting in the the grocery where liquor was sold, resolutions for or against slavery would excite passions. One can imagine disputes over any issue when feelings were at such a high pitch. These differences of opinion persisted quite some time in lower Illinois.

There is also a geographic reference to Pike County in the "Jim Bludso...." ballad which could escape notice. The Prairie Belle's competition in the great race was the "Movastar." ("The Movastar was the better boat, but the Prairie Belle she wouldn't be passed.") The name Movastar is a reference to Mauvaiseterre Creek which is near Naples and an Illinois River crossing. Abraham Lincoln, as a young attorney, crossed the river on his way to Pike County at this point, on his way to Pittsfield. The French word

THE PIKE COUNTY BALLADS

"mauvaiseterre" means red earth, and was applied to the the creek which flowed red with silt after a rain. Interestingly, Hay's spelling is also the Pike County pronunciation.

The Pike County Ballads have been left to us as a humorous, folksy reflection of those rural people who influenced the early life of John Hay. The characters in the ballads are strikingly close to the people who lived in and near Pike County, Illinois. The ballads are, I believe, based on people, places and events of this area.

                Warren D. Winston

                Pittsfield, Illinois

                December 2004

Publisher's Message

IN 2002 I traveled to Pike County, Illinois to introduce a book written long ago by Griggsville, Illinois resident John McWilliams, describing his experiences in the California Gold Rush and in the Civil War. At a meeting with members of the Pike County Historical Society, several people mentioned the work of another Pike County resident, John Hay. I discovered that Mr. Hay had written poetry, the *Pike County Ballads*. These poems were known as "dialect poetry" because the narrative was in the earthy colloquial speech of Southern Illinois of the period. Hay published the book in 1871, shortly after the Civil War. The language and culture of Pike County's population was at that time, to a significant degree, the result of immigration from Virginia, Kentucky and Tennessee.

THE PIKE COUNTY BALLADS

My curiosity piqued, I read the *Pike County Ballads*, and was delighted with the vigor, courage and foibles of the characters in the poems, however the use of the word "nigger" was enough to give me pause. James Stevenson Publisher's policy is not to publish works that insult or embarrass today's readers. It has been claimed that literature which carries forward ancient insults or slurs against any race or ethnic group perpetuates old stereotypes and that all books are not necessarily worthy of reprinting. I believe there must be some valuable historic material or significant literary merit in a candidate for reprinting, as in, for example, *Huckleberry Finn*. *Huckleberry Finn* contains the "n" word numerous times. There are African Americans who question the value of requiring students to read this classic of American literature because of its offensive language. This sensitivity should be addressed as one considers reprinting materials that might perpetuate prejudice.

PUBLISHER'S MESSAGE

When I was again asked about *The Pike County Ballads* this year, and took another look at it, I concluded that the good people of Pike County are right. This book of poetry holds a unique place in American literature, and does need to be available to today's reader. And what caused the change of heart?

Paul Findley, an untiring fan of Pike County, in a communication on another book expressed his very high regard for the Ballads. In view of Paul's enthusiasm, I re-read the poems with particular attention to "Banty Tim." This poem is a statement of a white man, Tilmon Joy, for his African American friend, Tim, a man who saved his life in the battle of Vicksburg. As I read the Ballads again, I became convinced that certainly Tilmon Joy's defense of his friend Tim was a good and honorable stand, however the *real* "hero" of the poem was Banty Tim. Tilmon Joy spoke on behalf of Banty Tim, whereas Tim risked his life, suffering several wounds on the battlefield, to save Sergeant Tilmon Joy, a truly heroic act. Viewing the poem in this light provided some balance for the appearance of the "n" word that still arouses feelings in many quarters in 2004. Language aside, Tim and Tilmon's friendship clearly transcended race - a friendship to which both were committed.

A closer look at the poem, "Banty Tim," may be of benefit. As Tilmon defends Tim, he quotes the "White Man's Committee of Spunky Point" saying, "And *whereas*, and *seein'*, and *wherefore*, The times being' all out o' jint, The nigger has got to mosey, From the limits of Spunky Point." Clearly these "*whereas*" and "*wherefore*" words of the White Man's Committee resolution do contain the word "nigger," however these are not the words of Tilmon Joy, he seems to be quoting. In the lines that follow, in each of his references, he uses Tim's name. As he recounts Tim's act of heroism in saving his life, he

PUBLISHER'S MESSAGE

pointedly says, "That nigger — *that Tim* — was a crawlin' to me, through that fire-proof, gilt-edged hell!" Tilmon's language highlights for his listeners, as he pauses in the story, his deliberate use of Tim's proper name. His clear choice to change from the derogatory "n" word, makes the point to readers that Tilmon chooses Tim's proper name to refer to his friend.

Another reason for my change of heart, as regards the value of producing the *Pike County Ballads*, is based on its place in the world of literature. There was a growing upheaval occurring in the literary world just after the Civil War. Hay's work broke new ground in challenging readers accustomed to a more genteel tradition in poetry and literature. Historian Kenton J. Clymer wrote an article in the *Missouri Historical Review* about John Hay and Mark Twain providing ample evidence for a lifetime friendship between the two men. Both Hay and Twain were

THE PIKE COUNTY BALLADS

aware of, and participated in, the changing literary fashion. Hay, as an Editor of the New York Tribune, was at the center of New York's literary scene in the post-bellum period. Correspondence shows that he actually assisted Twain by sending his writing to publishers for consideration, as in the case of his short work, *1601*. The two men were about the same age, and Hay used dialect extensively in his popular *Pike County Ballads* about the same time that Twain was writing *The Jumping Frog of Calaveras County* and *Innocents Abroad*.

In an article on the Internet adapted from a talk given at the July 1995 Summer Teachers' Institute at The Mark Twain House, Hartford, Connecticut, Dr. Shelley Fisher Fishkin wrote the following, "Something new happened in Huck Finn that had never happened in American literature before. ... *Huckleberry Finn* allowed a different kind of writing to happen: a clean, crisp, no-nonsense, earthy ver-

PUBLISHER'S MESSAGE

nacular kind of writing that jumped off the printed page with unprecedented immediacy and energy." Dr. Fishkin's adjectives are certainly fitting for Mark Twain's *Huckleberry Finn*, however she is not correct that this had never happened before. *Huckleberry Finn* was published in January 1885, fourteen years after the Ballads challenged readers used to a more genteel tradition in poetry and literature. In fact, even the earlier Tom Sawyer was written from 1872 to 1875 and was published in 1876. One would conclude that the *Pike County Ballads,* contemporaneous with Twain's earliest stories, and which was very popular in its day, does hold a special place in America's post-bellum literature, bringing authenticity through dialect and character, as readers were introduced to distant, rural American locales. John Hay was writing for an American audience using realism and naturalism in a manner that was carried forward by Twain.

THE PIKE COUNTY BALLADS

To some of our readers, this long statement in defense of *The Pike County Ballads* may seem to be unnecessary. There are those in our society, however, who might argue that Langston Hughes' commentary on the African Americans' feelings is still a powerful issue. At a Public Broadcasting System website which has a "Teacher's Guide" with the title, "Exploring the Controversy—The 'N' Word," Hughes is quoted regarding the use of "Nigger" in literature:

"Used rightly or wrongly, ironically or seriously, of necessity for the sake of realism, or impishly for the sake of comedy, it doesn't matter. Negroes do not like it in any book or play whatsoever, be the book or play ever so sympathetic in its treatment of the basic problems of the race. Even though the book or play is written by a Negro, they still do not like it. The word nigger, you see, sums up for us who are colored all the bitter years of insult and struggle in America."

PUBLISHER'S MESSAGE

...from a commentary in Hughes book, *The Big Sea*

These words were written in Hughes' memoirs in 1940. It is my belief that with the passing of sixty–five years, racist language is now universally condemned. One could argue that we gain nothing by hiding the faults of our past.

As we offer this new edition of Hay's ballads, I am confident that the literary world will recognize Hay's dialect poems for their significant place in American literary history, and will find them as worthy to be introduced to this generation as I have found them.

James Stevenson

Fairfield and Vacaville, California

December 2004

THE PIKE COUNTY BALLADS

Illustrator's Preface

Reeking with the swaggering spirit and customs of the early river-settlements along the Mississippi, the *Pike County Ballads* succeed pre-eminently in contemporizing the reader with those remote days. Living fragments lifted bodily and placed beneath our very eyes!

We hear the creak of wagons over the prairie roads; the lurch and strain of the stage-coach in the dark, the crack of the whip, and men's voices.

We are made to know that the sun flames upon the broad bosom of the Mississippi, and that the white, wheezing river-boats are gleaming on its surface, ever trailing their long waving banners of wood-smoke.

We hear the din of a fight in "Taggart's Hall"; we can smell the rum and tobacco, and note the glint of a quickly moving "Derringer" or the broad flash of a

THE PIKE COUNTY BALLADS

Bowie knife. We sense infinitely of these things.

And I have endeavored here to add my mite to these already potent lines; to lift the curtain intermittently, to draw the veil aside, cautiously, and look upon the unsuspecting folk of Pike County.

N.C. WYETH

Jim Bludso

*He weren't no saint, — them engineers
Is all pretty much alike*

JIM BLUDSO
of the
PRAIRIE BELLE

WALL, no! I can't tell whar he lives,
    Becase he don't live, you see;
Leastways, he's got out of the habit
    Of livin' like you and me.

Whar have you been for the last three year
    That you have n't heard folks tell
How Jimmy Bludso passed in his checks
    The night of the Prairie Belle?

He were n't no saint, — them engineers
    Is all pretty much alike, —

THE PIKE COUNTY BALLADS

One wife in Natchez-under-the-Hill

And another one here, in Pike;

A keerless man in his talk was Jim,

And an awkward hand in a row,

But he never flunked, and he never lied, —

I reckon he never knowed how.

And this was all the religion he had, —

To treat his engine well;

Never be passed on the river;

To mind the pilot's bell;

And if ever the Prairie Belle took fire, —

A thousand times he swore,

He'd hold her nozzle agin the bank

Till the last soul got ashore.

All boats has their day on the Mississip,

And her day come at last, —

The Movastar was a better boat,

But the Belle she *would n't* be passed.

JIM BLUDSO

And so she come tearin' along that night —
The oldest craft on the line —
With a nigger squat on her safety-valve,
And her furnace crammed, rosin and pine.

The fire bust out as she clared the bar,
And burnt a hole in the night,
And quick as a flash she turned, and made
For that willer-bank on the right.
There was runnin' and cursin', but Jim yelled out,
Over all the infernal roar,
"I'll hold her nozzle agin the bank
Till the last galoot's ashore."

Through the hot, black breath of the burnin' boat
Jim Bludso's voice was heard,
And they all had trust in his cussedness,
And knowed he would keep his word.
And, sure's you're born, they all got off
Afore the smokestacks fell, —

THE PIKE COUNTY BALLADS

And Bludso's ghost went up alone
In the smoke of the Prairie Belle.

He were n't no saint,— but at jedgment
I'd run my chance with Jim
'Longside of some pious gentlemen
That would n't shook hands with him.
He seen his duty, a dead-sure thing, —
And went for it thar and then;
And Christ ain't a going to be too hard
On a man that died for men.

Little Breeches

*No four-year-old in the county
Could beat him for pretty and strong*

LITTLE BREECHES

I DON'T go much on religion,
   I never ain't had no show;
But I've got a middlin' tight grip, sir,
   On the handful o' things I know.
I don't pan out on the prophets
And free-will, and that sort of thing, —
   But I b'lieve in God and the angels,
   Ever sence one night last spring.

I come into town with some turnips,
   And my little Gabe come along, —
   No four-year-old in the county
   Could beat him for pretty and strong,

THE PIKE COUNTY BALLADS

Peart and chipper and sassy,
Always ready to swear and fight, —
And I'd larnt him to chaw terbacker
Jest to keep his milk-teeth white.

The snow come down like a blanket
As I passed by Taggart's store;
I went in for a jug of molasses
And left the team at the door.
They scared at something and started, —
I heard one little squall,
And hell-to-split over the prairie
Went team, Little Breeches and all.

Hell-to-split over the prairie!
I was almost froze with skeer;
But we rousted up some torches,
And sarched for 'em far and near.
At last we struck hosses and wagon,
Snowed under a soft white mound,

JOHN HAY: AUTHOR AND STATEMAN

Upsot, dead beat, — but of little Gabe
No hide nor hair was found.
And here all hope soured on me,
Of my fellow-critter's aid, —
I jest flopped down on my marrow-bones,
Crotch-deep in the snow, and prayed.

● ● ● ● ● ● ● ● ●

By this, the torches was played out,
And me and Isrul Parr
Went off for some wood to a sheepfold
That he said was somewhar thar.

We found it as last, and a little shed
Where they shut up the lambs at night.

THE PIKE COUNTY BALLADS

We looked in and seen them huddled thar,

So warm and sleepy and white;

And THAR sot Little Breeches and chirped,

As peart as ever you see,

"I want a chaw of terbacker,

And that's what's the matter of me."

How did he git thar? Angels.

He could never have walked in that storm.

They jest scooped down and toted him

To whar it was safe and warm.

And I think that saving a little child,

And fotching him to his own,

Is a derned sight better business

Than loafing around The Throne.

*But he staggered up, and packed me off,
With a dozen stumbles and falls*

BANTY TIM

(REMARKS OF SERGEANT TILMON JOY TO THE WHITE MAN'S COMMITTEE OF SPUNKY POINT, ILLINOIS.)

I RECKON I git your drift, gents, —
You 'low the boy sha'n't stay;
This is a white man's country;
You're dimocrats, you say;
And whereas, and seein', and wherefore,
The times bein' all out o' j'int,
The nigger has got to mosey
From the limits o' Spunky P'int!

Le's reason the thing a minute:
I'm an old-fashion Dimocrat too,

THE PIKE COUNTY BALLADS

Though I laid my politics out o' the way

For to keep till the war was through.

But I come back here, allowin'

To vote as I used to do,

Though it gravels me like the devil to train

Along o' sich fools as you.

Now dog my cats ef I kin see,

In all the light of the day,

What you've got to do with the question

Ef Tim shill go or stay.

And furder than that I give notice,

Ef one of you tetches the boy,

He kin check his trunks to a warmer clime

Than he 'll find in Illanoy.

Why, blame your hearts, jest hear me!

You know that ungodly day

When our left struck Vicksburg Heights, how ripped

and torn and tattered we lay.

BANTY TIM

When the rest retreated I stayed behind,
    Fur reasons sufficient to me, —
With a rib caved in, and a leg on a strike,
    I sprawled on that cursed glacee.

Lord! how hot the sun went for us,
    And br'iled and blistered and burned!
How the Rebel bullets whizzed round us
    When a cuss in his death-grip turned!
Till along toward dusk I seen a thing
    I could n't believe for a spell:
That nigger — that Tim — was a crawlin' to me
    Through that fire-proof, gilt-edged hell!

The Rebels seen him as quick as me,
    And the bullets buzzed like bees;
But he jumped for me, and shouldered me,
    Though a shot brought him once to his knees;
But he staggered up, and packed me off,
    With a dozen stumbles and falls,

THE PIKE COUNTY BALLADS

Till safe in our lines he drapped us both,
His black hide riddled with balls.

So, my gentle gazelles, thar's my answer,
And here stays Banty Tim:
He trumped Death's ace for me that day,
And I'm not goin' back on him!
You may rezoloot till the cows come home,
But ef one of you tetches the boy,
He'll wrastle his hash to-night in hell,
Or my name's not Tilmon Joy!

The Mystery of Gilgal

I ax yer parding, Mister Phinn —
Jest drap that whisky-skin

The MYSTERY of GILGAL

The darkest, strangest mystery
　　I ever read, or heern, or see,
Is 'long of a drink at Taggart's Hall, —
　　Tom Taggart's of Gilgal.

I've heern the tale a thousand ways,
　　But never could git through the maze
That hangs around that queer day's doin's;
　　But I'll tell the yarn to youans.

Tom Taggart stood behind his bar,
　　The time was fall, the skies was fa'r
The neighbors round the counter drawed,
　　And ca'mly drinked and jawed.

At last come Colonel Blood of Pike,

And old Jedge Phinn, permiscus-like,

And each, as he meandered in,

Remarked, "A whisky-skin."

Tom mixed the beverage full and fa'r,

And slammed it smoking, on the bar.

Some says three fingers, some says two, —

I'll leave the choice to you.

Phinn to the drink put forth his hand;

Blood drawed his knife, with accent bland,

I ax yer parding, Mister Phinn —

Jest drap that whisky-skin."

No man high-toneder could be found

Than old Jedge Phinn the country round.

Says he, "Young man, the tribe of Phinns

Knows their own whisky-skins!"

He went for his "leven-inch bowie-knife: —

"I tries to foller a Christian life;

But I'll drap a slice of liver or two,

My bloomin' shrub, with you."

They carved in a way that all admired,

Tell Blood drawed iron at last, and fired.

It took Seth Bludso 'twixt the eyes,

Which caused him great surprise.

THE PIKE COUNTY BALLADS

Then coats went off, and all went in;
Shots and bad language swelled the din;
The short, sharp bark of Derringers,
Like bull-pups, cheered the furse.

They piled the stiffs outside the door;
They made, I reckon, a cord or more.
Girls went that winter, as a rule,
Alone to spellin'-school.

I've sarched in vain from Dan to Beer-
Sheba, to make this mystery clear;
But I end with *hit* as I did begin, —
"WHO GOT THE WHISKY-SKIN?"

Golyer

Over hill and holler and ford and creek
Jest like the hosses had wings, we tore

GOLYER

E F the way a man lights out of this world
   Helps fix his heft for the other sp'ere,
I reckon my old friend Golyer's Ben

Will lay over lots of likelier men

For one thing he done down here.

You did n't know Ben? He driv a stage

On the line they called the Old Sou'west;

He wa'n't the best man that ever you seen,

And he wa'n't so ungodly pizen mean, —

No better nor worse than the rest.

THE PIKE COUNTY BALLADS

He was hard on women and rough on his friends;

And he did n't have many, I'll let you know;

He hated a dog and disgusted a cat,

But he'd run off his legs for a motherless brat,

And I guess there's many jess so.

I've seed my sheer of the run of things,

I've hoofed it a many and many a miled,

But I never seed nothing that could or can

Jest git all the good from the heart of a man

Like the hands of a little child.

Well! this young one I started to tell you about, —

His folks was all dead, I was fetchin' him

through, —

GOLYER

He was just at the age that's loudest for boys,
And he blowed such a horn with his sarchin' small voice,
We called him "the Little Boy Blue."

He ketched a sight of Ben on the box,
And you bet he bawled and kicked and howled,
For to git 'long of Ben, and ride thar too;
I tried to tell him it would n't do,
When suddenly Golyer growled,

What's the use of making the young one cry?
Say, what the use of being a fool?
Sling the little one up here whar he can see,
He won't git the snuffles a-ridin' with me, —
The night ain't any too cool."

THE PIKE COUNTY BALLADS

The child hushed cryin' the minute he spoke;

"Come up here, Major! don't let him slip."

And jest as nice as a woman would do,

He wropped his blanket around them two,

And was off in the crack of a whip.

We rattled along an hour or so,

Till we heerd a yell on the still night air.

Did you ever hear an Apache yell?

Well, ye need n't want to, *this* side of hell;

There's nothing more devilish there.

Caught in the shower of lead and flint

We felt the old stage stagger and plunge;

Then we heerd the voice and the whip of Ben,

As he gethered his critters up again,

And tore away with a lunge.

The passengers laughed. "Old Ben's all right,

He's druv five year and never was struck."

GOLYER

"Now if *I*'d been thar, as sure as you live,
They'd a plugged me with holes as thick as
a sieve;
It's the reg'lar Golyer luck."

Over the hill and holler and ford and creek
Jest like the hosses had wings, we tore;
We got to Looney's and Ben come in
And laid down the baby and axed for his gin,
And dropped in a heap on the floor.

Said he, "When they fired, I kivered the kid, —
Although I ain't pretty, I'm middlin' broad;

THE PIKE COUNTY BALLADS

And look! he ain't fazed by arrow nor ball, —

Thank God! my own carcase stopped them all."

Then we seen his eye glaze, and his lower jaw

fall, —

And he carried his thanks to God.

The Pledge at Spunky Point

*The Deacon and Parson Skeeters
In the tail of a game of Draw*

A TALE OF EARNEST EFFORT AND HUMAN PERFIDY

IT'S all very well for preaching',
   But preachin and practice don't gee
I've give the thing a fair trial,
   And you can't ring it in on me.
So toddle along with your pledge, Squire,
   Ef that's what you want me to sign;
Betwixt me and you, I've been thar,
   And I'll not take any in mine.

A year ago last Fo'th July

A lot of the boys was here.

THE PIKE COUNTY BALLADS

We all got corned and signed the pledge

For to drink no more that year.

There was Tilmon Joy and Sheriff McPhail

And me and Abner Fry,

And Shelby's boy Leviticus

And the Golyers, Luke and Cy.

And we anteed up a hundred

In the hands of Deacon Kedge

For to be divided the follerin' Fo'th

"Mongst the boys that kep' the pledge.

And we knowed each other so well, Squire,

You may take my scalp for a fool,

Ef every man when he signed his name

Did n't feel cock-sure of the pool.

Fur a while it all went lovely;

We put up a job next day.

Fur to make Joy b'lieve his wife was dead,

And he went home middlin' gay;

THE PLEDGE AT SPUNKY POINT

Then Abner Fry he killed a man,
And afore he was hung McPhail
Jest bilked the widder outen her sheer
By getting him slewed in jail.

But Chris'mas scooped the Sheriff,
The egg-nogs gethered him in;
And Shelby's boy Leviticus
Was, New Year's, tight as sin;
And along in March the Golyers
Got so drunk that a fresh-biled owl
Would 'a' looked, 'long-side o' them two young men,
Like a sober temperance fowl.

THE PIKE COUNTY BALLADS

Four months alone I walked the chalk,
I thought my heart would break;
And all them boys a-slappin' my back
And axin', "What'll you take?"
I never slep' without dreamin' dreams
Of Burbin, Peach, or Rye,
But I chawed at my niggerhead and swore
I'd rake that pool or die.

At last — the Fo'th — I thumped myself
Through chores and breakfast soon,
Then scooted down to Taggarts' store —
For the pledge was off at noon;
And all the boys was gethered thar,
And each man hilt his glass —
Watchin' me and the clock quite solemn-like
Fur to see the last minute pass.

The clock struck twelve! I raised the jug
And took one lovin pull —

THE PLEDGE AT SPUNKY POINT

I was holler clar from skull to boots,

It seemed I could n't git full.

But I was roused by a fiendish laugh

That might have raised the dead —

Them ornary sneaks had sot the clock

a half an hour ahead!

"All right!" I squawked. "You've got me,

Jest order your drinks agin,

And we'll paddle up to the Deacon's

And scoop the ante in."

But when we got to Kedge's,

What a sight was that we saw!

The Deacon and Parson Skeeters

In the tail of a game of Draw.

They had shook 'em the heft of the mornin',

The Parson's luck was fa'r,

And he raked, the minute we got thar,

The last of our pool on a pa'r.

THE PIKE COUNTY BALLADS

So toddle along with your pledge, Squire,

I 'low it's all very fine,

But ez fur myself, I thank ye,

I'll not take any in mine.

The End

History books by
James Stevenson Publisher
www.jspub.com

A. Lincoln: The Crucible of Congress
Former Congressman Paul Findley
(Listed in Burkhimer's *100 Essential Lincoln Books*)

Victory at Sea
Rear Admiral William Sowden Sims
Pulitzer Prize winning story of WWI U-boat warfare

Ranch Life & The Hunting Trail—
Theodore Roosevelt

Our Pike County, The Soul of Western Illinois
Carol McCartney

Grape Culture, Wines and Winemaking
Agoston Haraszthy's 1861 report of the beginning of California's wine industry—with foreword by Dr. Stephen Krebs

Humbugs & Heroes, A Gallery of California Pioneers
Richard H. Dillon

Spanish Hill - Gold Hill
Archeological story of mining camps in the Gold Rush period

The Life of Mrs. Robert Louis Stevenson
Nellie Van de Grift Sanchez

Stevenson at Silverado
Ann Roller Issler
The reports of people who knew R.L. Stevenson, from his honeymoon period in Calistoga, California with wife, Fanny.

Recollections of John McWilliams
Autobiography
Griggsville, Illinois resident's Gold Rush & Civil War memories

Six Months in the Gold Mines
E. Gould Buffum
Bancroft called this book, "One of the most important contributions to the history of California."

Joe's Luck
Horatio Alger
Reprint of a classic Horatio Alger story of an orphan who goes to California, and through hard work and good luck, makes his fortune

Also children's California history books

California Beginnings
Lola Hoffman
A children's reader about life in California under Spain and Mexico

*California Missions -
History and Model Building Ideas for Children*
Don Baxter

California History for Children
Edited by James Stevenson

Natalie Hernandez's
popular three part series about famous Californians
Stowaway to California! - the story of Father Serra,
Captain Sutter's Fort and
Mapmakers of the Western Trails, Adventures with John Fremont

These and other history books sold at
www.jspub.com online bookstore,
Barnes and Noble online or Amazon.com
and select bookstores everywhere

Printed in the United States
43332LVS00003B/415-420